"And in the end it is not the years in your life that count, it's the life in your years."

Abraham Lincoln

"Time does not always pass at the same speed. We are the ones that determine that speed."

Paulo Coehlo

For A.L.T.
3/23/2016

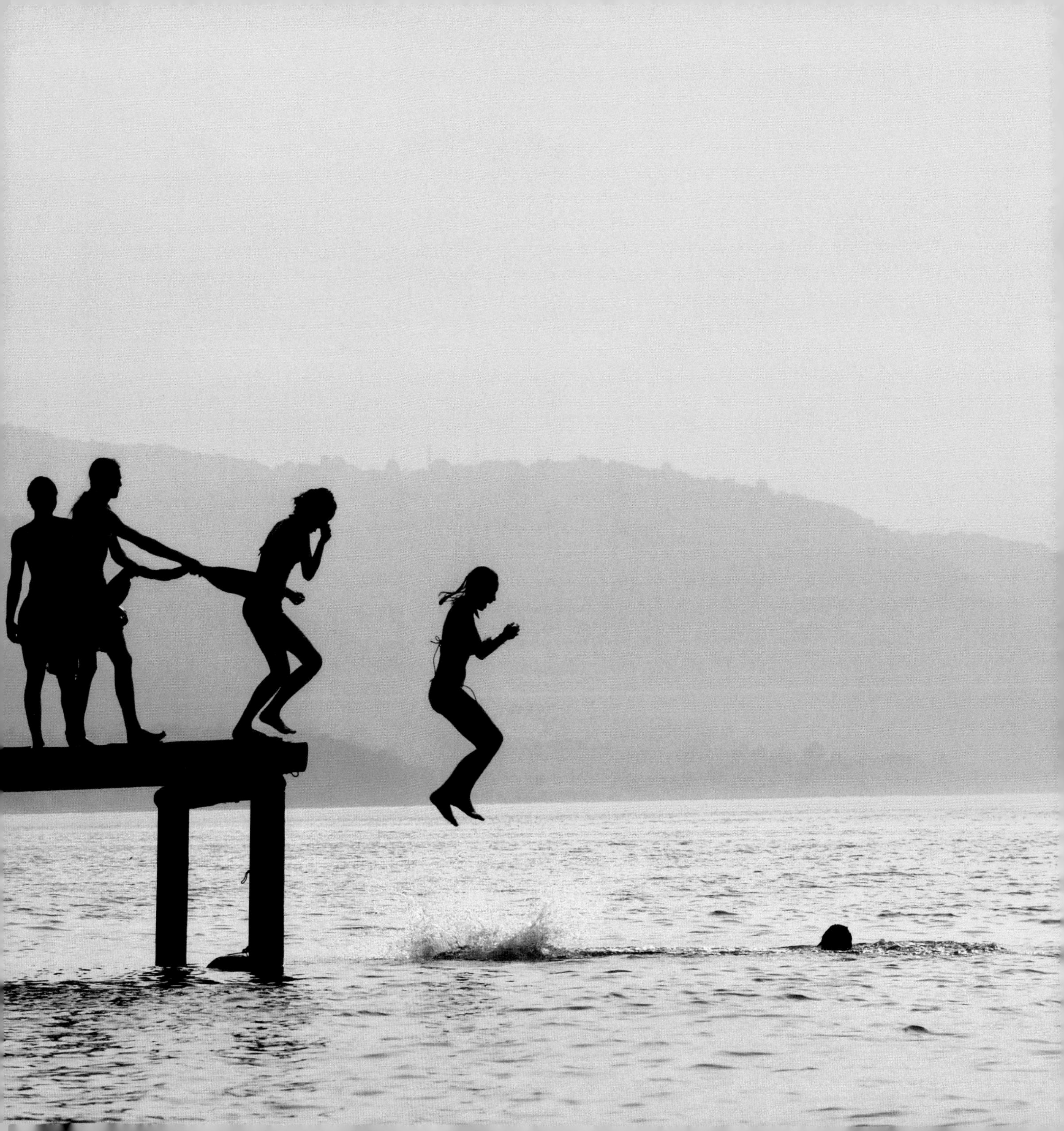

How long did summers last as a kid?

Splashing into the lake, riding bikes across busy streets

Crushes, broken hearts, bruises and dirty knees

We all know summer lasted "forever" as a kid

Everything was new – we **really lived** everything we did

And now? How long do they last, in this world of the mundane?

I don't know about you but I *ache* to live endless summers again.

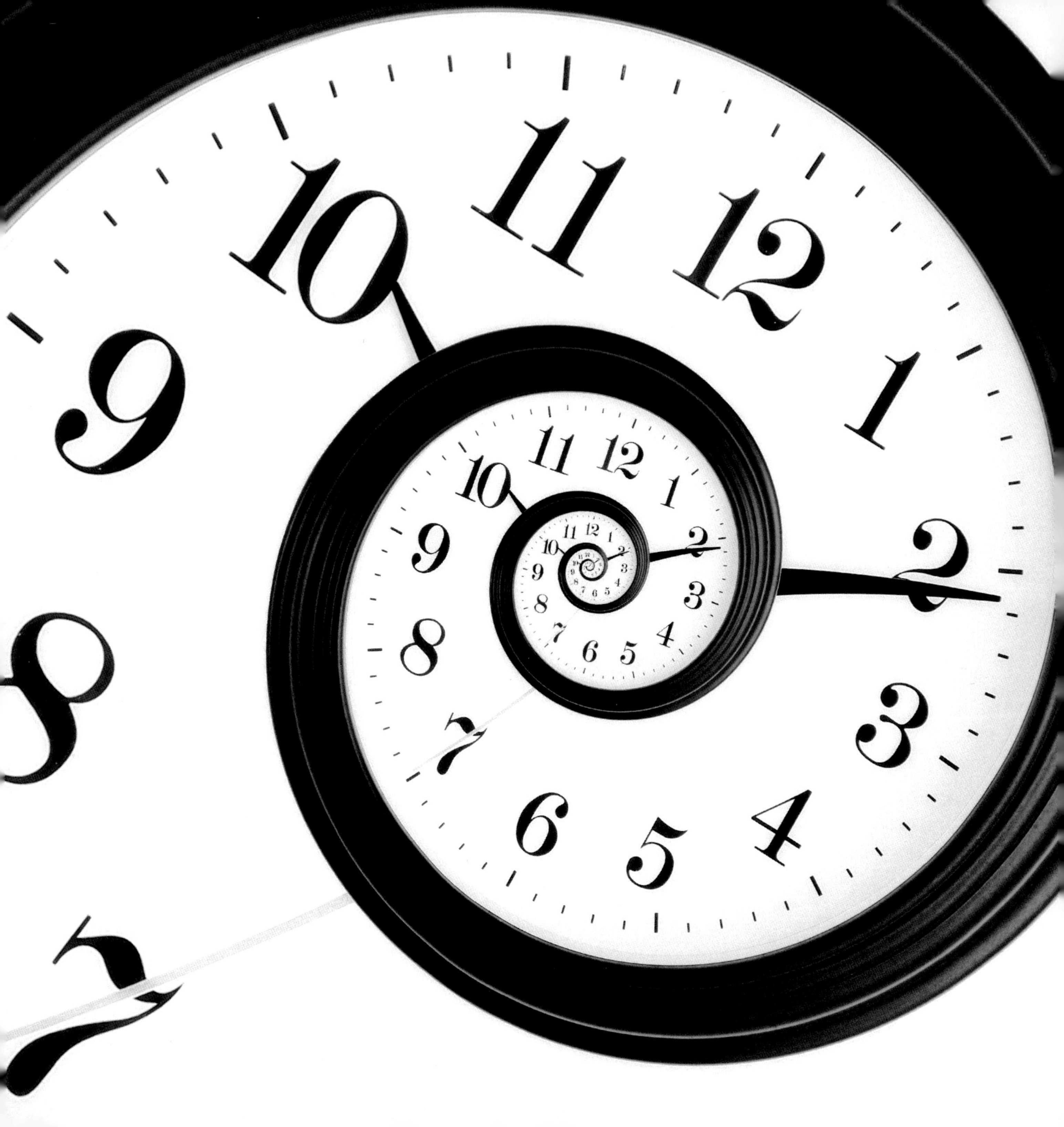

This thing here, it's a lie

We've been lied to, side-tracked, distracted, manipulated

This ticking, this tocking

This terrible terminal tracking of the ticking of time teaching us trivial untruths

It taught us that each second is exactly the same

That each minute, each hour, each day, progresses in a linear way

And that each is the same distance from the last

That these ticks and these tocks are an accurate measure of our past.

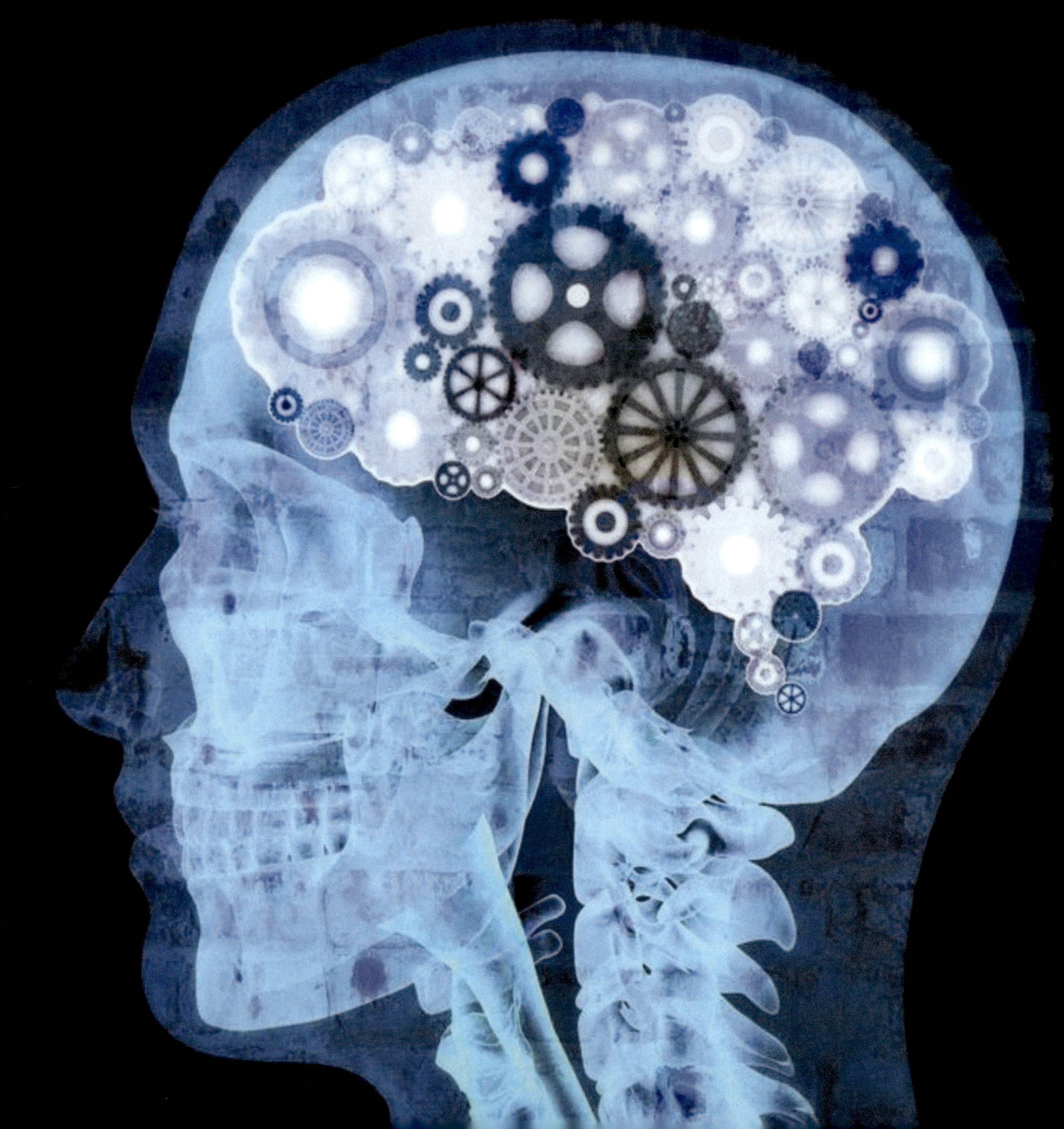

This thing here, your brain, is quite different than this thing that we call a clock

As it turns out, this thing called a brain isn't run by a clock

Or more accurately it has many clocks like these all running at different speeds

Time in our brains doesn't tick-tock tick-tock with equal density

Time in our brains is dependent on our experiences

And their **relative intensity.**

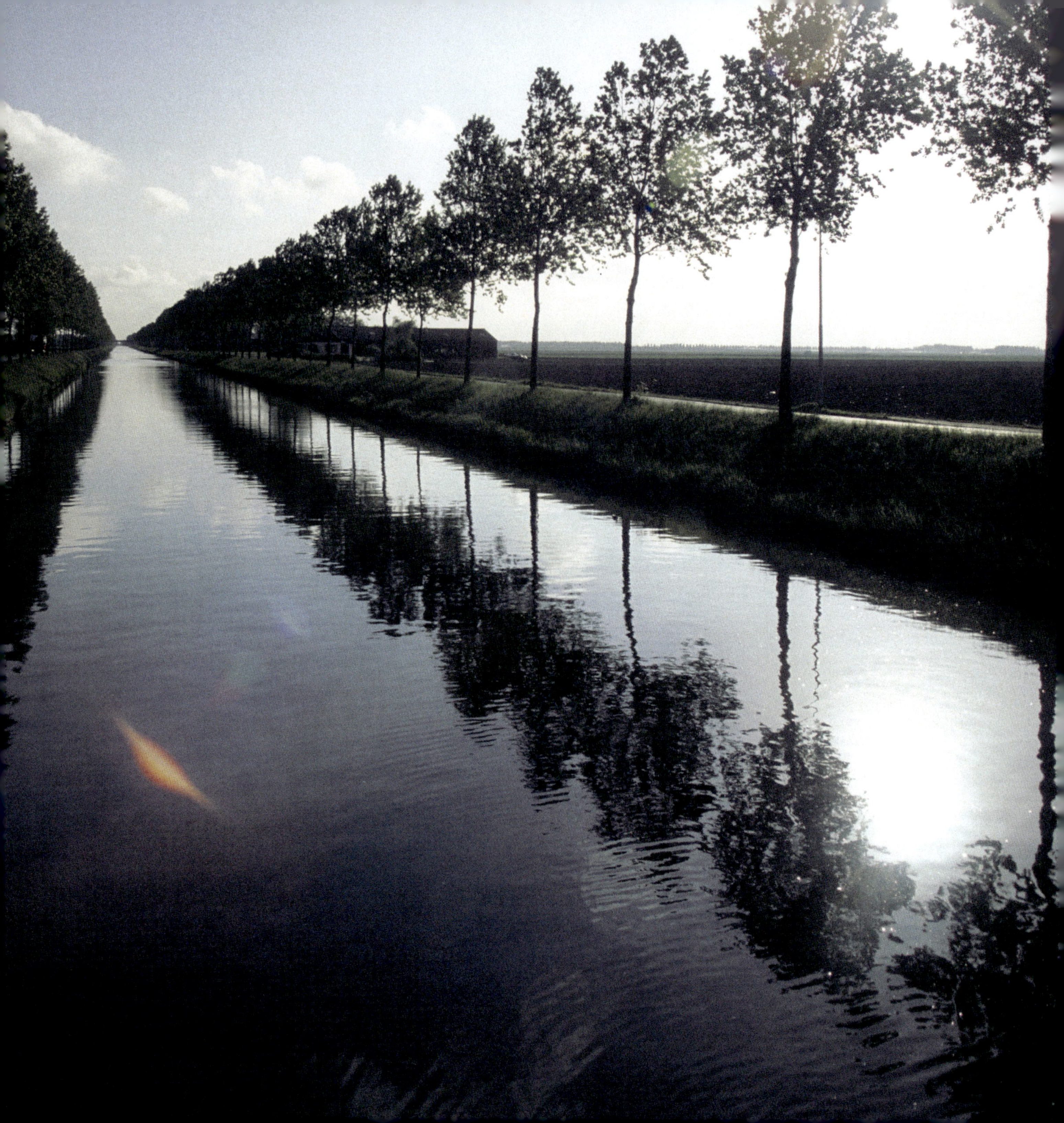

But wait, time, time is like a river, right?

Sure time is a river all right

But not this kind of river.

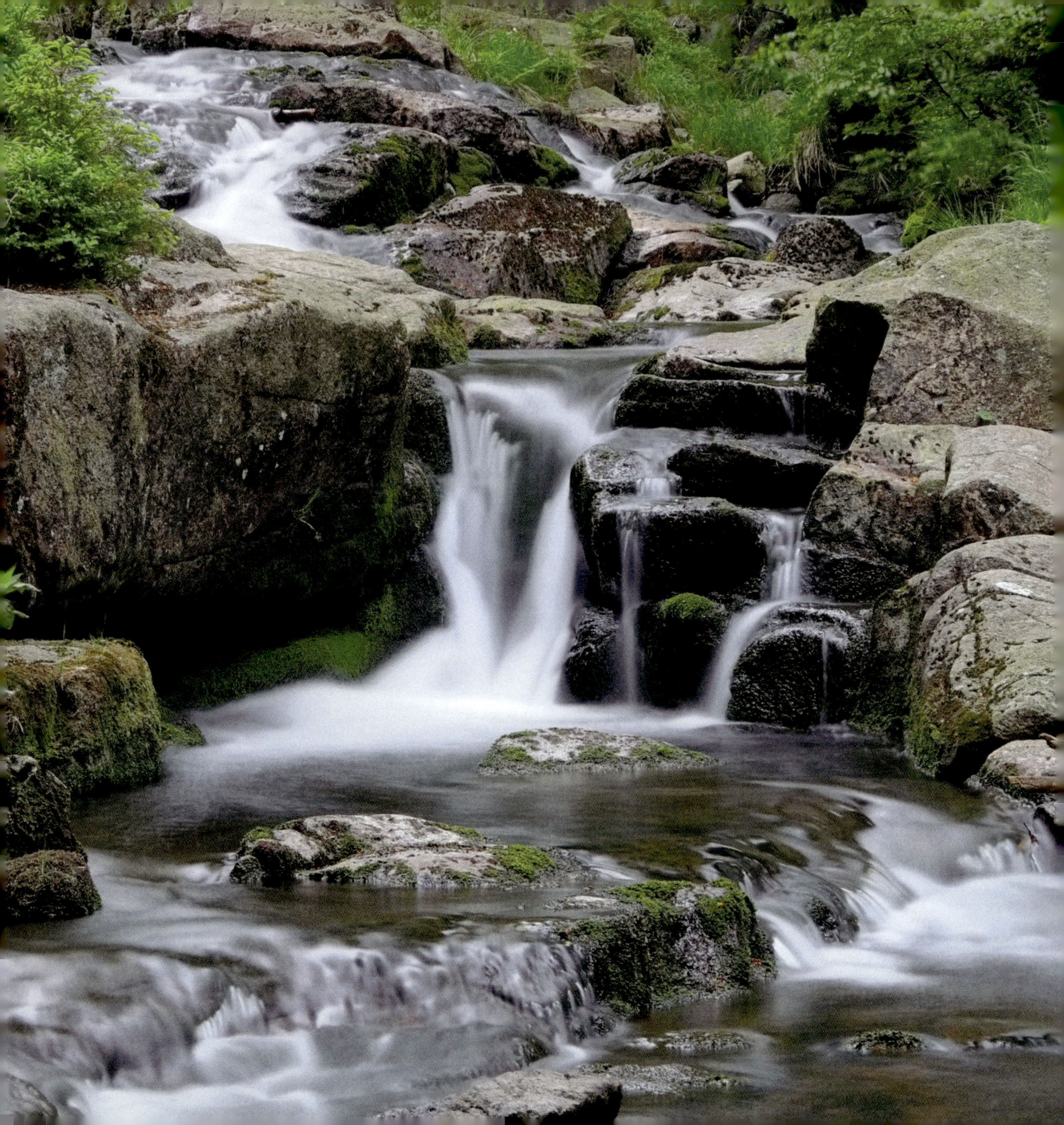

No, time is river that ebbs and flows

From trickles to rapids, waterfalls and pools

They bend, they bow, they curve, they dry up

In the brain it is the same game

The river of time is to blame

The fact is, we don't experience time always the same.

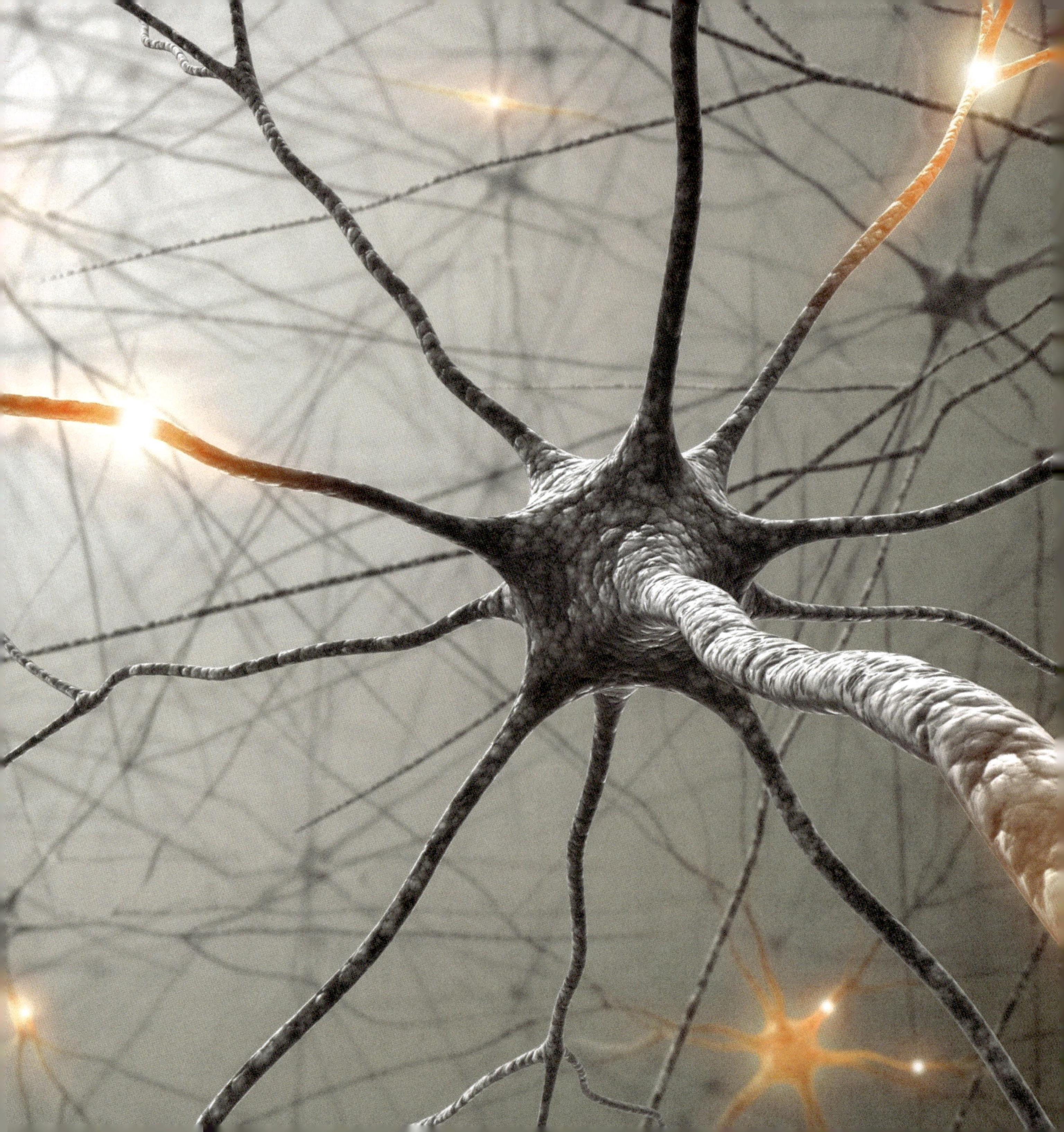

Neuroscientists tell us that the experience of time is relative

And that the drivers behind its flexibility are by their nature cognitive

Kahneman calls it, "thinking fast and slow"

Csikszentmihalyi, he calls it "Flow"

Regardless, it is a paradox we all know

That when time accelerates in the present

It expands in retro.

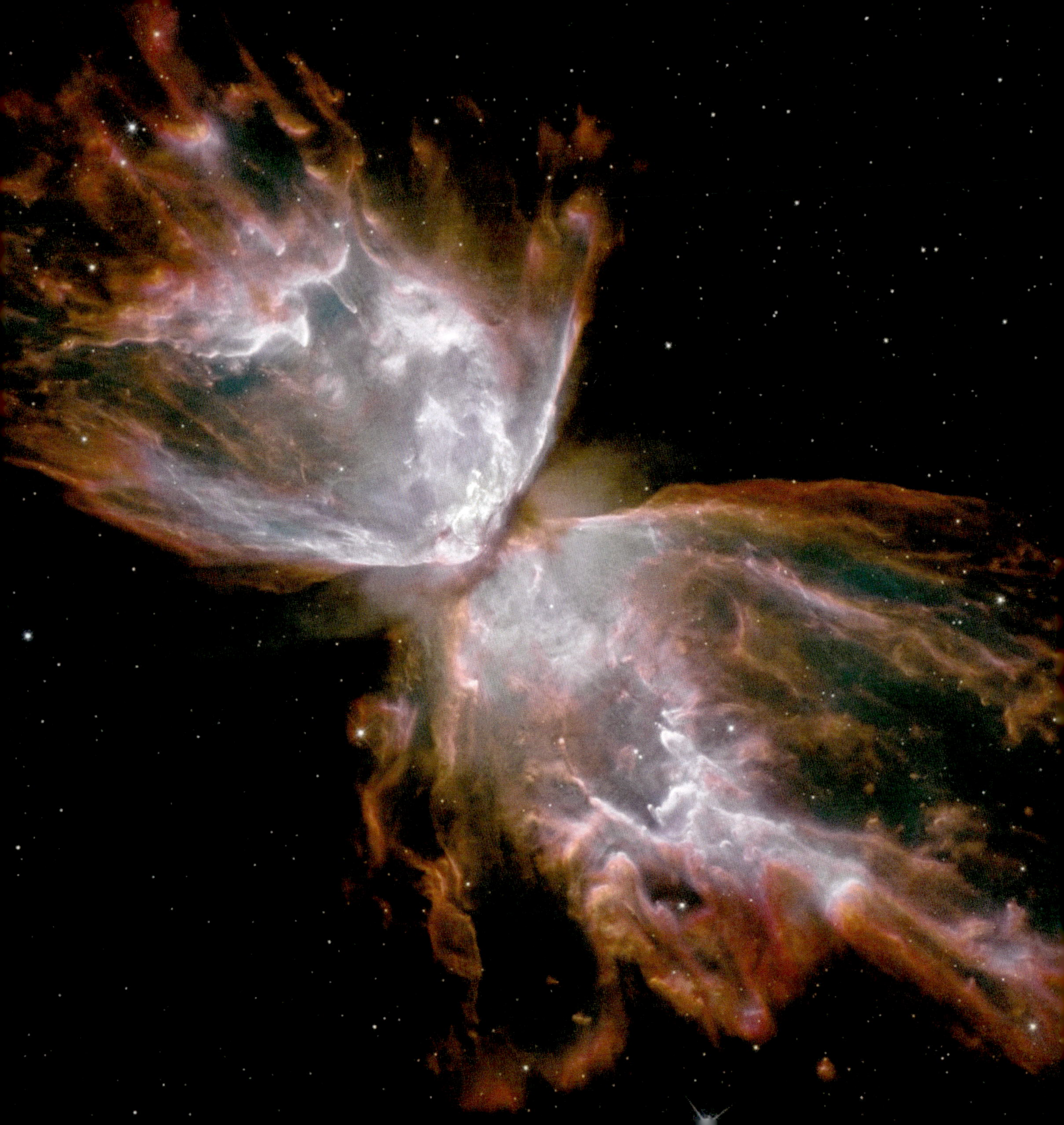

Physics teaches us the theory of relativity

In a massive gravitational pull there's a change in activity

As you accelerate towards the speed of light

There is an **"event horizon"** where you lose all sight.

Time inside stops relative to the outside world

Under the massive forces and compression even time itself is swirled.

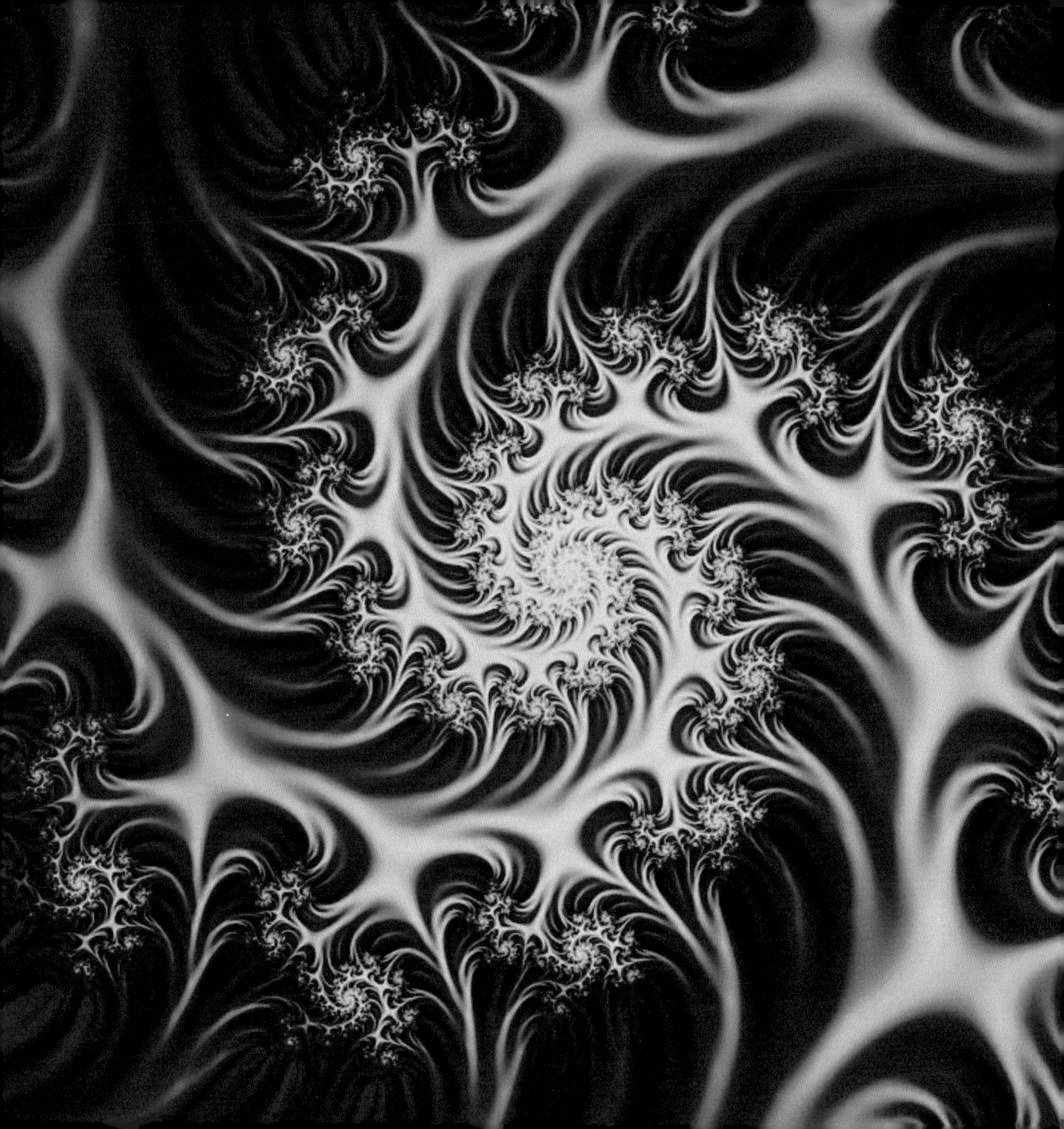

It is a slinky on a staircase, a complex **blue fractal**

It's a Copernican rollercoaster, string theory in a cat's cradle

It is bellows and helixes and event horizons at the ends

Time stops when it speeds up, it decelerates when it bends.

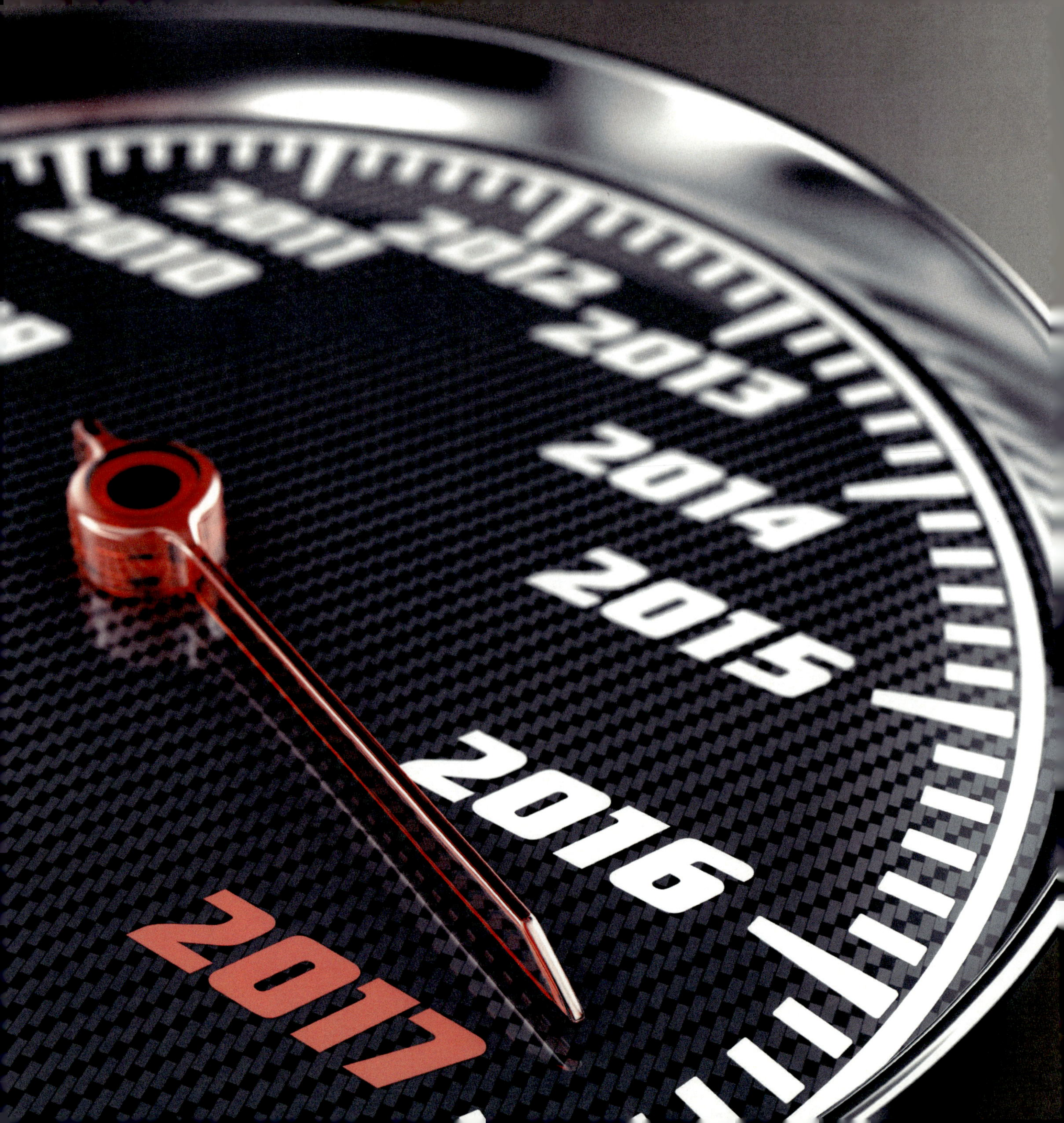
2010
2011
2012
2013
2014
2015
2016
2017

What about your life – is time speeding up or slowing down?

98% of adults feel life is accelerating

I don't know about you, but that makes me frown

How is that OK?

Who ordered the code red? *(and who let Tom Cruise in this monologue? He's too short – just like your life)*

You want the truth? You can't handle the truth

Here's your code red, here's the truth:

Experiential time, absent aggressive action to reverse it, will keep speeding up.

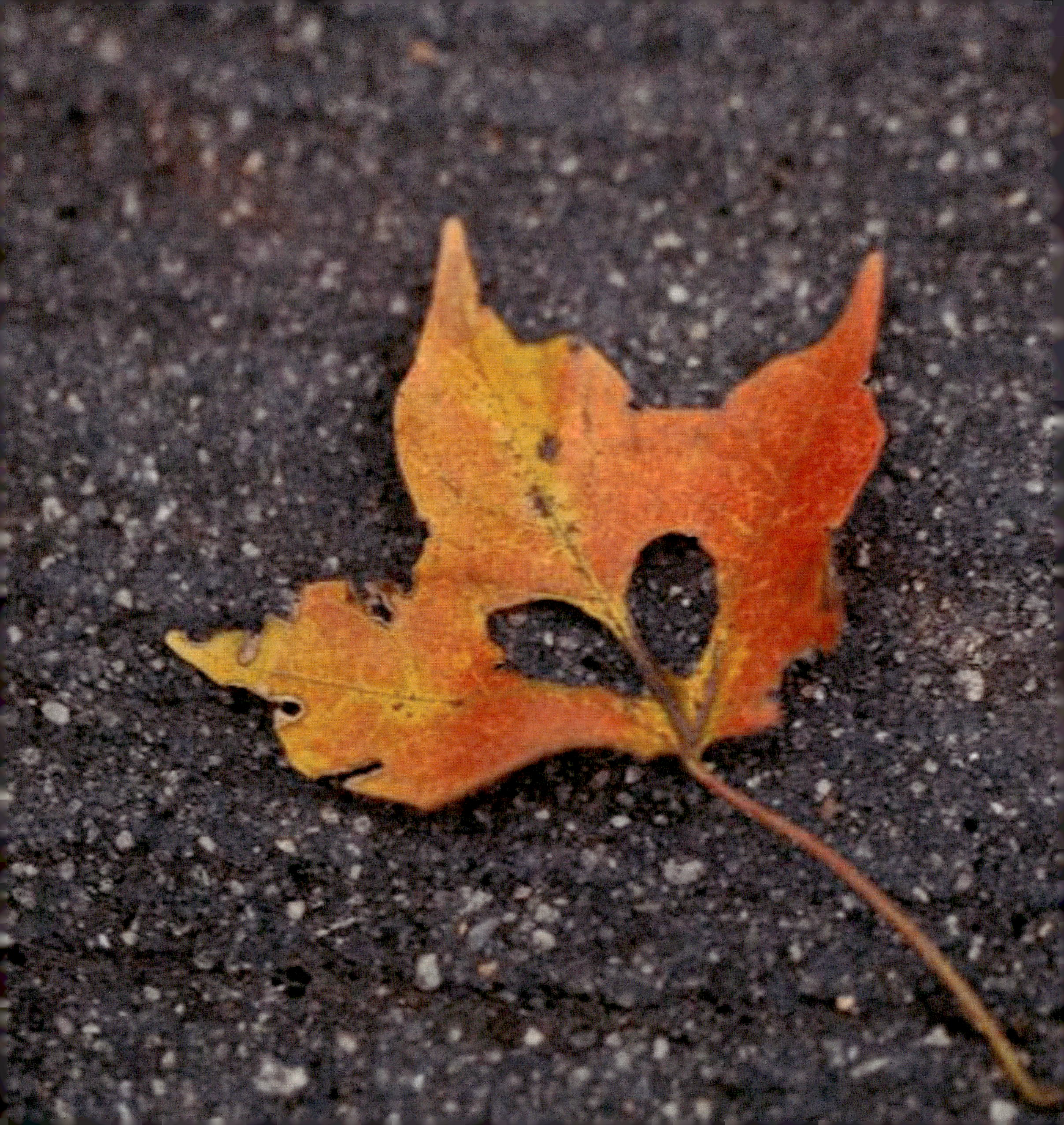

So . . . go ahead, avoid the highs and lows of life

And here's what you are going to get:

Each September will come faster

Leaves piled at your feet

And no one, **no one** will warm you

Or sing you to sleep

Want to speed through life with nothing to remember?

Here's how to reap another pale September:

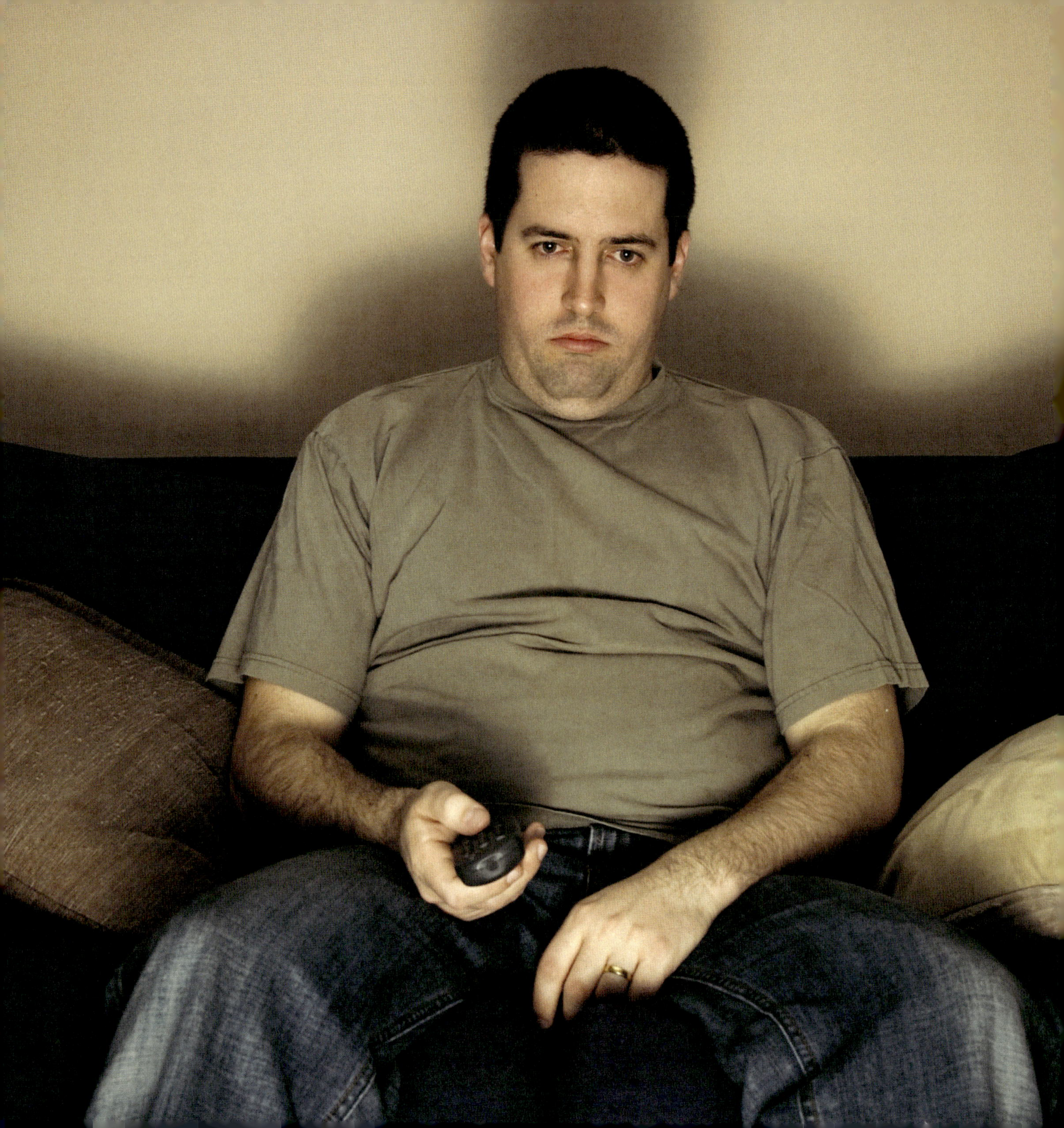

Watch lots of TV, sit on the couch,

Eat the same foods, develop a pouch

Meet no new friends, be a stay at home grouch

Do the same damn thing every single day, walk with a slouch

Your arm chair? The gauze of Advil, Paxil and air conditioning?

Your staid routines and complacent pace?

These things are the warp drive to temporal hyperspace.

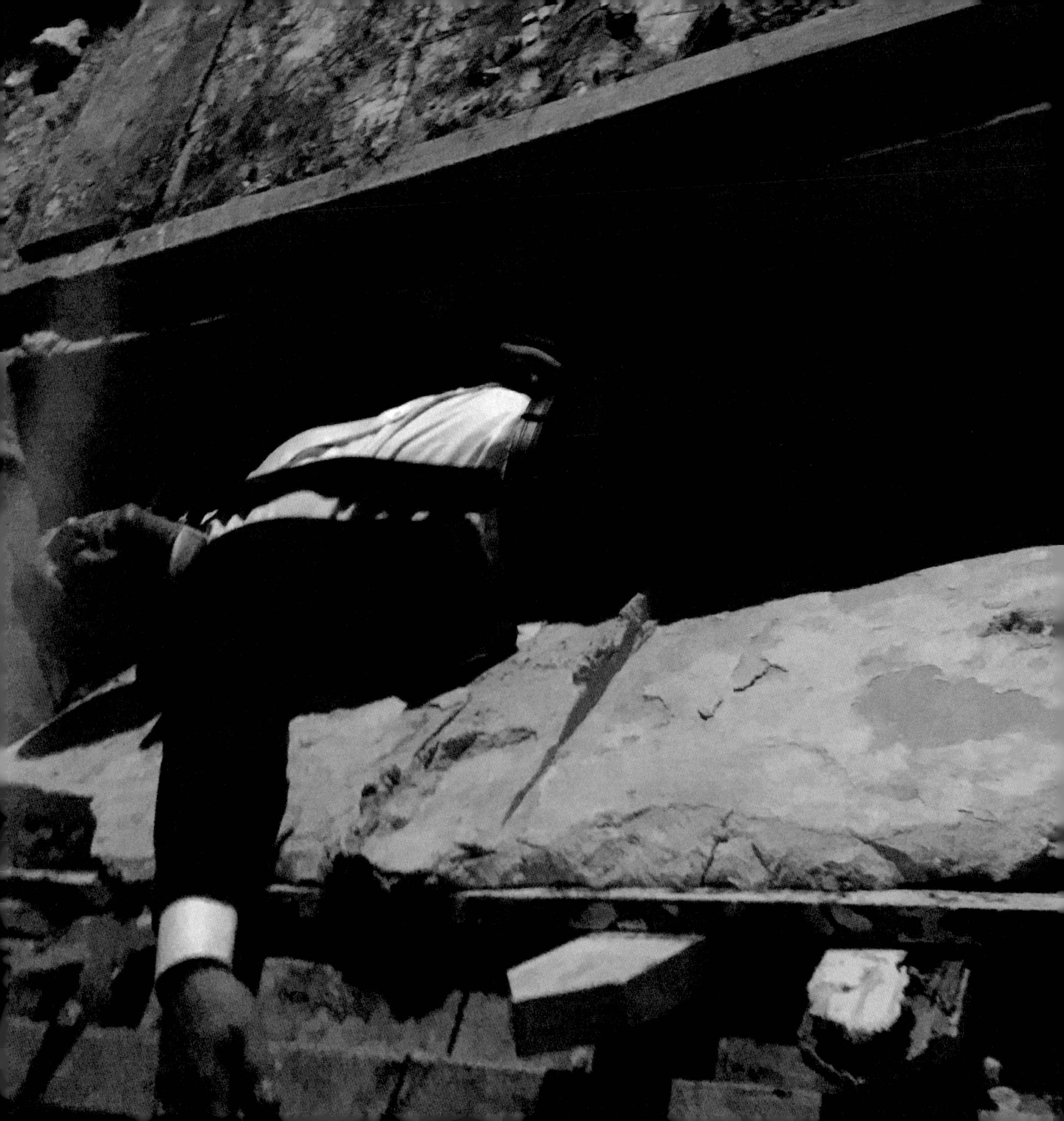

You think you are half done with life or even less?

No, only a small percent of your experiential time is left for you to save

You have one foot, a torso, two hands, and a watch in the grave

Be safe, stick with your routine

Be comfortable, live "the dream"

And die in a few temporal seconds

Goodnight, you're dead

End . . . of . . . scene . . .

Photo credit: Katelina Lola Coyle

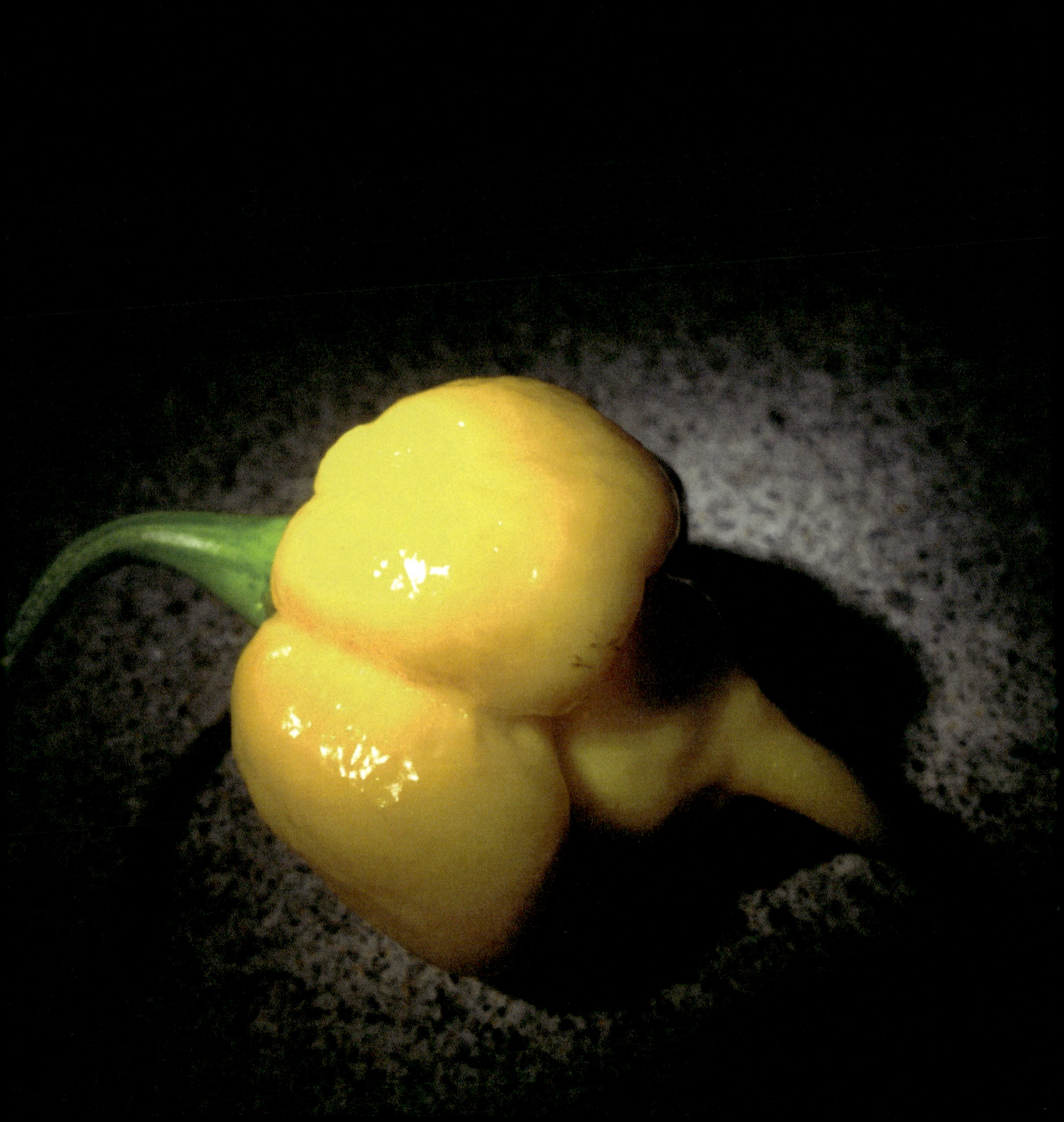

It is time.

It is time to either get busy dying

Or get busy **really living**

It is time to get dirty, to get sick, to burnout and recover

It is time too fall in love, to have a broken heart

To fall apart and then get back up again

Time to eat a Moruga Scorpion pepper without milk.

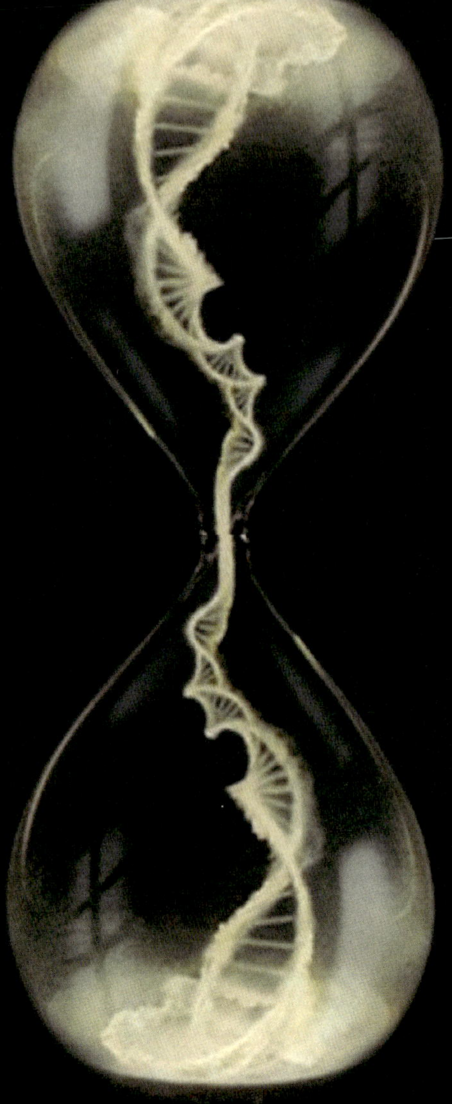

It is time to get back out there, get back in there

Time to get off the hedonic treadmill

Time to un-climb the corporate ladder

I want to climb the ladder of my internal clock

I want to clock the ladder of my internal climb

I want to slow the hands of father time

And time the slow hands of my fatherhood.

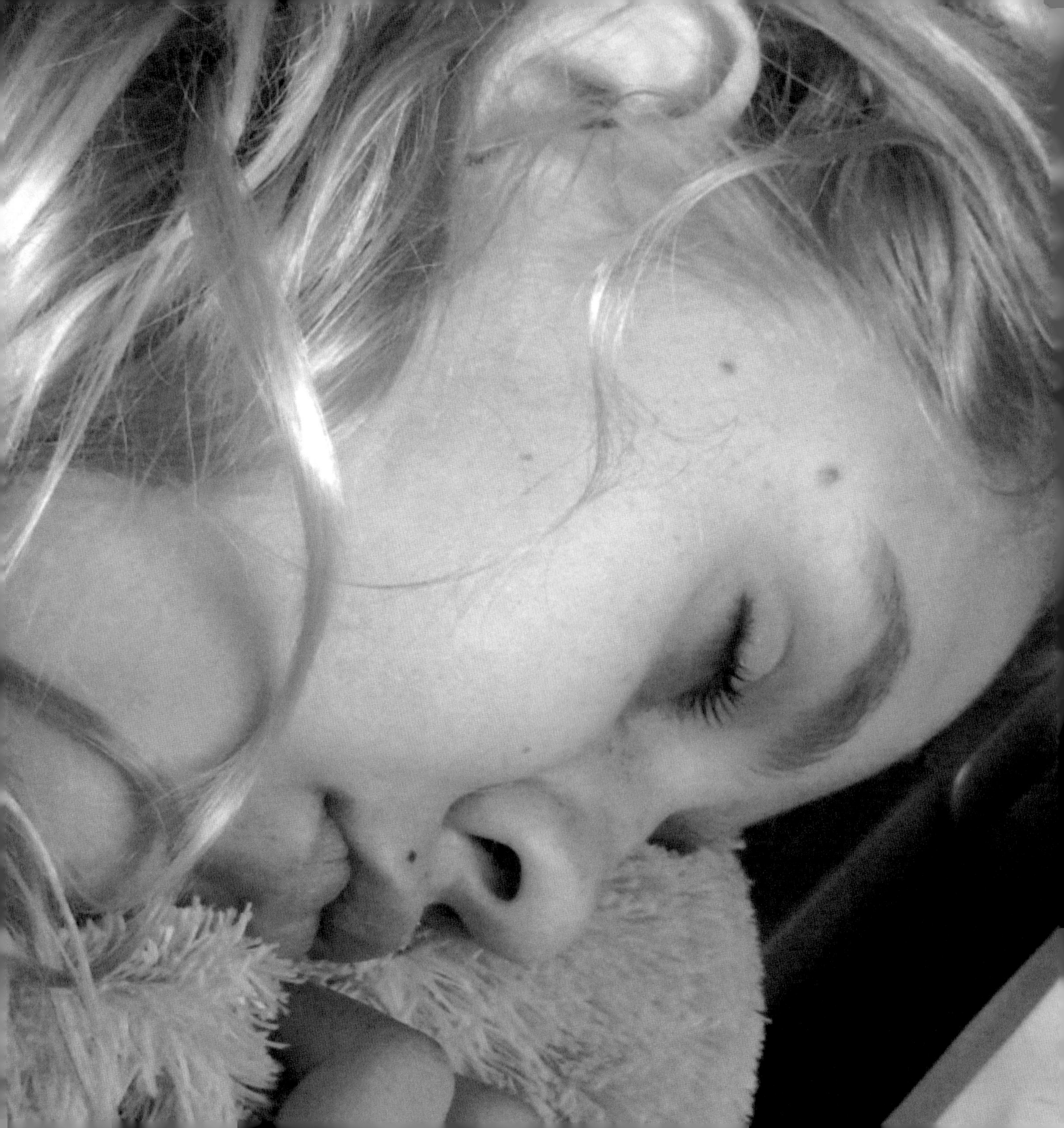

I want to kiss my young child's forehead, and wake to find her still a child

I want to love the love of my life, and live a life that I love

I want to sleep the dreams of heroes, and be the hero of my dreams

I accept this kind of life may mean suffering for me

I will choose this suffering, rather than let it choose me.

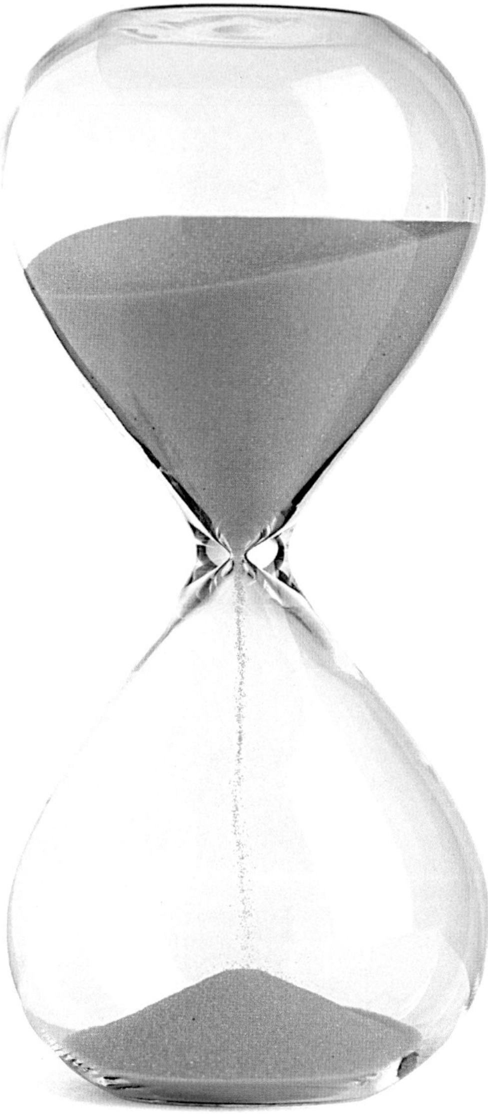

It is time.

It is time to create moments of such gravity

Where meaning supersedes all

It is time . . . to create event horizons

Where the clock ceases to exist at all

For the people we truly love, this one sacred gift we can give

The gift of expanding time

It is time:

to "really live."

About The Art of Really Living Movement

Why: I believe that time is our most valuable commodity. I believe that the way we experience time is not linear and that our perceptions of time are strongly influenced by the stories we tell, and the meaning we make. I believe we can innovate the human experience and expand time in the process.

I believe that - absent action to correct it - each summer will feel shorter than the last, and that life is not just short, it is actively getting shorter. I believe that there is a way to slow, stop and reverse the perceived acceleration of time and live summers longer than when we were kids: but it is not easy.

I believe that by designing lives focused on our strengths, we can increase our resilience and take on larger challenges, face bigger risks and create more memories. I believe that we can innovate our lives to avoid the malaise of modernity, avoid the stifling conventions and muffling routines that lead to small risks, small rewards and a lack of meaning.

The mission of "The Art of Really Living" is to expand our experience with time by designing indelible time-stopping moments. These "event horizon moments" play the role of the chrysalis, breaking the clay of grey men, revealing the colors of the sleeping poet, mathematician, painter, scientist, athlete or musician within.

About the Author

John K. Coyle, Founder of The Art of Really Living, is one of the world's leading experts in innovation and Design Thinking. He is a graduate of Stanford University's "d.school" where his guidance counselor was David Kelley, the founder of IDEO and Steve Jobs' right hand man. John earned his MBA from Northwestern University's Kellogg Graduate School of Management, and has been applying "design thinking" to innovate companies, careers, lives, and leadership challenges for more than 20 years.

John is a thought leader in the field of horology – the study of how we as humans process time. He is a two time TEDx presenter, an NBC Sports analyst, SVP and Professor of Innovation, author and sought-after keynote speaker. John is also an Olympic medalist - an achievement he attributes directly to his design thinking background.

John's talent is weaving facts, frameworks and storytelling into experiential learning sessions that activate both the intellectual and emotional centers for participants.

JohnKCoyle.com

Made in the USA
Middletown, DE
02 January 2025